D0344553

MADE

FOR

HEAVEN

AND WHY ON EARTH
IT MATTERS

C. S. LEWIS

 HarperSanFrancisco
A Division of HarperCollinsPublishers

CONTENTS

INTRODUCTION

Heaven is always with us. That is
one of the richest themes running
through the writings of Clive Staples
(C. S.) Lewis, the late Cambridge
professor of literature and one of the
most influential (and perhaps least
likely) writers on faith and Christianity in the twentieth century. With an
uncanny knack for communicating
seemingly complicated spiritual

truths in a way both the curious and the devout can understand, Lewis brings the lofty subject of heaven to our front door by explaining how every action we take moves us closer either to heaven or to its opposite.

But these riches are sprinkled throughout his works. Here we have gathered three selections where Lewis addresses the nature of heaven directly and which offer a more thorough presentation of his thoughts on the topic than readers could get from any one book.

First, in *The Great Divorce,* Lewis takes people on a fanciful bus trip from hell to heaven, where any of the travelers may stay if they so choose. Here Lewis explores a truly revolutionary idea: perhaps the gates of hell are locked from the *inside*. Ultimately, we choose whether we want to live in heaven or in hell. Lewis's preface, which we have included here, explains the either-or of heaven: "If we insist on keeping Hell (or even Earth) we shall not see Heaven: if we accept Heaven we shall not be able to retain even the smallest and most intimate souvenirs of Hell."

In Lewis's rich meditation on suffering in *The Problem of Pain,* he reveals how our very desire for heaven makes our experience of pain a problem that demands an explanation. In his chapter on "Heaven," Lewis writes of our deep unfulfilled longing: "We cannot tell each other about it. It is the secret signature of each soul, the incommunicable and unappeasable want, the thing we wanted before we met our wives or made our friends or chose our work, and which we shall still desire on our deathbeds, when the mind no longer knows wife or friend or work. While we are, this is. If we lose this, we lose all."

Many people point to C. S. Lewis's sermon "Weight of Glory" as his most profound meditation on heaven, including this oft-quoted passage on how our ultimate destinies should inform our daily interactions with others: "It is a serious thing to live in a society of possible gods and goddesses, to remember that the dullest and most uninteresting person you can talk to may one day be a creature which, if you saw it now, you would be strongly tempted to worship, or else a horror and a corruption such as you now meet, if at all, only in a nightmare. All day long we are, in some degree, helping each other to one or the other of these destinations."

In the end Lewis takes us far beyond the simple Sunday-school lessons on heaven and into the deep mysteries heaven was meant to signify. As the children run up the mountain of Aslan's country in *The Last Battle* and as the characters shout at the end of *The Great Divorce,* so Lewis takes us "further up and further in" to that sweet, sweet reality called heaven.

—*The Editors*

MADE

FOR

HEAVEN

I

PREFACE TO
THE GREAT
DIVORCE

BLAKE WROTE the Marriage of Heaven and Hell. If I have written of their Divorce, this is not because I think myself a fit antagonist for so great a genius, nor even because I feel at all sure that I know what he meant. But in some sense or other the attempt to make that marriage is perennial. The attempt is based on the belief that reality never presents us with an

(Taken from The Great Divorce, *C. S. Lewis's classic account of a bus trip from hell to heaven with the promise that the visitors from hell may stay if they choose to.)*

absolutely unavoidable 'either-or';
that, granted skill and patience and
(above all) time enough, some way of
embracing both alternatives can always be found; that mere develop-
ment or adjustment or refinement
will somehow turn evil into good
without our being called on for a
final and total rejection of anything
we should like to retain. This belief I
take to be a disastrous error. You cannot take all luggage with you on all
journeys; on one journey even your
right hand and your right eye may be
among the things you have to leave
behind. We are not living in a world

where all roads are radii of a circle
and where all, if followed long
enough, will therefore draw gradually
nearer and finally meet at the centre:
rather in a world where every road,
after a few miles, forks into two, and
each of those into two again, and at
each fork you must make a decision.
Even on the biological level life is not
like a river but like a tree. It does not
move towards unity but away from it
and the creatures grow further apart
as they increase in perfection. Good,
as it ripens, becomes continually
more different not only from evil but
from other good.

I do not think that all who choose
wrong roads perish; but their rescue
consists in being put back on the
right road. A sum can be put right:
but only by going back till you find
the error and working it afresh from
that point, never by simply *going on*.
Evil can be undone, but it cannot
'develop' into good. Time does not
heal it. The spell must be unwound,
bit by bit, 'with backward mutters of
dissevering power'—or else not. It is
still 'either-or'. If we insist on keeping Hell (or even Earth) we shall not
see Heaven: if we accept Heaven we
shall not be able to retain even the

smallest and most intimate souvenirs
of Hell. I believe, to be sure, that any
man who reaches Heaven will find
that what he abandoned (even in
plucking out his right eye) has not
been lost: that the kernel of what he
was really seeking even in his most
depraved wishes will be there, beyond
expectation, waiting for him in 'the
High Countries'. In that sense it will
be true for those who have com-
pleted the journey (and for no others)
to say that good is everything and
Heaven everywhere. But we, at this
end of the road, must not try to anticipate that retrospective vision. If

we do, we are likely to embrace the
false and disastrous converse and
fancy that everything is good and
everywhere is Heaven.

But what, you ask, of earth? Earth,
I think, will not be found by anyone
to be in the end a very distinct place.
I think earth, if chosen instead of
Heaven, will turn out to have been,
all along, only a region in Hell: and
earth, if put second to Heaven, to
have been from the beginning a part
of Heaven itself.

There are only two things more to
be said about this small book. Firstly,
I must acknowledge my debt to a

writer whose name I have forgotten
and whom I read several years ago in
a highly coloured American magazine
of what they call 'Scientifiction'.
The unbendable and unbreakable
quality of my heavenly matter was
suggested to me by him, though he
used the fancy for a different and
most ingenious purpose. His hero
travelled into the *past:* and there, very
properly, found raindrops that would
pierce him like bullets and sand-
wiches that no strength could bite—
because, of course, nothing in the
past can be altered. I, with less origi-
nality but (I hope) equal propriety;

have transferred this to the eternal.
If the writer of that story ever reads
these lines I ask him to accept my
grateful acknowledgement. The
second thing is this. I beg readers to
remember that this is a fantasy. It
has of course—or I intended it to
have—a moral. But the transmortal
conditions are solely an imaginative
supposal: they are not even a guess
or a speculation at what may actually
await us. The last thing I wish is to
arouse factual curiosity about the
details of the after-world.

—*C. S. Lewis*
April, 1945

2

HEAVEN

It is required
You do awake your faith.
Then all stand still;
Or those that think it is
unlawful business
I am about, let them depart.

—SHAKESPEARE,
Winter's Tale

Plunged in thy depth of
mercy let me die
The death that every soul
that lives desires.

—COWPER,
out of *Madame Guion*

I RECKON,' said St Paul, 'that the sufferings of this present time are not worthy to be compared with the glory that shall be revealed in us.'* If this is so, a book on suffering which says nothing of heaven, is leaving out almost the whole of one side of the account. Scripture and tradition habitually

(Taken from Chapter 10 of The Problem of Pain by C. S. Lewis)

*Romans 8:18.

put the joys of heaven into the scale
against the sufferings of earth, and
no solution of the problem of pain
which does not do so can be called a
Christian one. We are very shy nowa-
days of even mentioning heaven. We
are afraid of the jeer about 'pie in the
sky', and of being told that we are
trying to 'escape' from the duty of
making a happy world here and now
into dreams of a happy world elsewhere. But either there is 'pie in the
sky' or there is not. If there is not,
then Christianity is false, for this
doctrine is woven into its whole fab-
ric. If there is, then this truth, like

any other, must be faced, whether it
is useful at political meetings or no.
Again, we are afraid that heaven is a
bribe, and that if we make it our goal
we shall no longer be disinterested. It
is not so. Heaven offers nothing that
a mercenary soul can desire. It is safe
to tell the pure in heart that they shall
see God, for only the pure in heart
want to. There are rewards that do
not sully motives. A man's love for a
woman is not mercenary because he
wants to marry her, nor his love for
poetry mercenary because he wants
to read it, nor his love of exercise less
disinterested because he wants to run

and leap and walk. Love, by definition, seeks to enjoy its object.

You may think that there is another
reason for our silence about heaven—
namely, that we do not really desire it.
But that may be an illusion. What I
am now going to say is merely an
opinion of my own without the
slightest authority, which I submit to
the judgement of better Christians
and better scholars than myself. There
have been times when I think we do
not desire heaven; but more often I
find myself wondering whether, in
our heart of hearts, we have ever desired anything else. You may have noticed that the books you really love are

bound together by a secret thread. You
know very well what is the common
quality that makes you love them,
though you cannot put it into words:
but most of your friends do not see it
at all, and often wonder why, liking
this, you should also like that. Again,
you have stood before some landscape,
which seems to embody what you
have been looking for all your life; and
then turned to the friend at your side
who appears to be seeing what you
saw—but at the first words a gulf
yawns between you, and you realise
that this landscape means something
totally different to him, that he is pur-
suing an alien vision and cares nothing

for the ineffable suggestion by which
you are transported. Even in your
hobbies, has there not always been
some secret attraction which the others
are curiously ignorant of—something,
not to be identified with, but always
on the verge of breaking through, the
smell of cut wood in the workshop
or the clap-clap of water against the
boat's side? Are not all lifelong friendships born at the moment when at last
you meet another human being who
has some inkling (but faint and uncertain even in the best) of that something which you were born desiring,
and which, beneath the flux of other
desires and in all the momentary

silences between the louder passions, night and day, year by year, from childhood to old age, you are looking for, watching for, listening for? You have never *had* it. All the things that have ever deeply possessed your soul have been but hints of it—tantalising glimpses, promises never quite fulfilled, echoes that died away just as they caught your ear. But if it should really become manifest—if there ever came an echo that did not die away but swelled into the sound itself—you would know it. Beyond all possibility of doubt you would say 'Here at last is the thing I was made for.' We cannot tell each other about it. It is the secret signature of each soul, the incommunicable and unappeasable want, the thing we desired before we met our wives or made our friends or chose our work, and which we shall still desire on our deathbeds, when the mind no longer knows wife or friend or work. While we are, this is. If we lose this, we lose all.*

This signature on each soul may be a product of heredity and environment, but that only means that heredity and environment are among

---

*I am not, of course, suggesting that these immortal longings which we have from the Creator because we are men, should be confused with the gifts of the Holy Spirit to those who are in Christ. We must not fancy we are holy because we are human.

the instruments whereby God creates
a soul. I am considering not how,
but why, He makes each soul unique.
If He had no use for all these differ-
ences, I do not see why He should
have created more souls than one. Be
sure that the ins and outs of your in-
dividuality are no mystery to Him;
and one day they will no longer be a
mystery to you. The mould in which
a key is made would be a strange
thing, if you had never seen a key:
and the key itself a strange thing if
you had never seen a lock. Your soul
has a curious shape because it is a
hollow made to fit a particular
swelling in the infinite contours of

the Divine substance, or a key to un-
lock one of the doors in the house
with many mansions. For it is not humanity in the abstract that is to be
saved, but you—you, the individual
reader, John Stubbs or Janet Smith.
Blessed and fortunate creature, your
eyes shall behold Him and not another's. All that you are, sins apart, is
destined, if you will let God have His
good way, to utter satisfaction. The
Brocken spectre 'looked to every
man like his first love', because she
was a cheat. But God will look to
every soul like its first love because
He is its first love. Your place in

heaven will seem to be made for you and you alone, because you were made for it—made for it stitch by stitch as a glove is made for a hand.

It is from this point of view that we can understand hell in its aspect of privation. All your life an unattainable ecstasy has hovered just beyond the grasp of your consciousness. The day is coming when you will wake to find, beyond all hope, that you have attained it, or else, that it was within your reach and you have lost it forever.

This may seem a perilously private and subjective notion of the pearl of

great price, but it is not. The thing I
am speaking of is not an experience.
You have experienced only the *want*
of it. The thing itself has never actually been embodied in any thought,
or image, or emotion. Always it has
summoned you out of yourself. And
if you will not go out of yourself to
follow it, if you sit down to brood on
the desire and attempt to cherish it,
the desire itself will evade you. 'The
door into life generally opens behind
us' and 'the only wisdom' for one
'haunted with the scent of unseen
roses, is work.'* This secret fire goes

---

*George MacDonald, Alec Forbes, cap. xxxiii.

out when you use the bellows: bank
it down with what seems unlikely
fuel of dogma and ethics, turn your
back on it and attend to your duties,
and then it will blaze. The world is
like a picture with a golden back-
ground, and we the figures in that
picture. Until you step off the plane
of the picture into the large dimen-
sions of death you cannot see the
gold. But we have reminders of it. To
change our metaphor, the blackout is
not quite complete. There are chinks.
At times the daily scene looks big
with its secret.

Such is my opinion; and it may be
erroneous. Perhaps this secret desire

also is part of the Old Man and must
be crucified before the end. But this
opinion has a curious trick of evad-
ing denial. The desire—much more
the satisfaction—has always refused to
be fully present in any experience.
Whatever you try to identify with it,
turns out to be not it but something
else: so that hardly any degree of cru-
cifixion or transformation could go
beyond what the desire itself leads us
to anticipate. Again, if this opinion is
not true, something better is. But
'something better'—not this or that
experience, but beyond it—is almost
the definition of the thing I am trying to describe.

The thing you long for summons you away from the self. Even the desire for the thing lives only if you abandon it. This is the ultimate law—the seed dies to live, the bread must be cast upon the waters, he that loses his soul will save it. But the life of the seed, the finding of the bread, the recovery of the soul, are as real as the preliminary sacrifice. Hence it is truly said of heaven 'in heaven there is no ownership. If any there took upon him to call anything his own, he would straightway be thrust out into hell and become an evil spirit.'* But

---

* *Theologia Germanica*, li.

it is also said 'To him that overcometh
I will give a white stone, and in the
stone a new name written, which no
man knoweth saving he that receiveth
it.'* What can be more a man's own
than this new name which even in
eternity remains a secret between
God and him? And what shall we take
this secrecy to mean? Surely, that
each of the redeemed shall forever
know and praise some one aspect of
the Divine beauty better than any
other creature can. Why else were
individuals created, but that God,

---

*Revelation 2:17.

loving all infinitely, should love each
differently? And this difference, so far
from impairing, floods with meaning
the love of all blessed creatures for
one another, the communion of the
saints. If all experienced God in
the same way and returned Him an
identical worship, the song of the
Church triumphant would have no
symphony, it would be like an or-
chestra in which all the instruments
played the same note. Aristotle has
told us that a city is a unity of un-
likes,* and St Paul that a body is a

---

* *Politics,* ii, 2, 4.

unity of different members.* Heaven
is a city, and a Body, because the
blessed remain eternally different: a
society, because each has something
to tell all the others—fresh and ever
fresh news of the 'My God' whom
each finds in Him whom all praise as
'Our God'. For doubtless the continually successful, yet never complete,
attempt by each soul to communicate
its unique vision to all others (and
that by means whereof earthly art
and philosophy are but clumsy imita-
tions) is also among the ends for
which the individual was created.

---

* 1 Corinthians 12:12–30.

For union exists only between distincts; and, perhaps, from this point of view, we catch a momentary glimpse of the meaning of all things. Pantheism is a creed not so much false as hopelessly behind the times. Once, before creation, it would have been true to say that everything was God. But God created: He caused things to be other than Himself that, being distinct, they might learn to love Him, and achieve union instead of mere sameness. Thus He also cast His bread upon the waters. Even within the creation we might say that inanimate matter, which has no will, is one with God in a sense in which

men are not. But it is not God's purpose that we should go back into that
old identity (as, perhaps, some Pagan
mystics would have us do) but that
we should go on to the maximum
distinctness there to be reunited with
Him in a higher fashion. Even within
the Holy One Himself, it is not suf-
ficient that the Word should *be* God,
it must also be *with* God. The Father
eternally begets the Son and the
Holy Ghost proceeds: deity intro-
duces distinction within itself so that
the union of reciprocal loves may
transcend mere arithmetical unity or
self-identity.

But the eternal distinctness of each soul—the secret which makes of the union between each soul and God a species in itself—will never abrogate the law that forbids ownership in heaven. As to its fellow-creatures, each soul, we suppose, will be eternally engaged in giving away to all the rest that which it receives. And as to God, we must remember that the soul is but a hollow which God fills. Its union with God is, almost by definition, a continual self-abandonment— an opening, an unveiling, a surrender, of itself. A blessed spirit is a mould ever more and more patient of the

33

bright metal poured into it, a body ever more completely uncovered to the meridian blaze of the spiritual sun. We need not suppose that the necessity for something analogous to self-conquest will ever be ended, or that eternal life will not also be eternal dying. It is in this sense that, as there may be pleasures in hell (God shield us from them), there may be something not all unlike pains in heaven (God grant us soon to taste them).

For in self-giving, if anywhere, we touch a rhythm not only of all creation but of all being. For the Eternal Word also gives Himself in sacrifice;

and that not only on Calvary. For
when He was crucified He 'did that
in the wild weather of His outlying
provinces which He had done at
home in glory and gladness'.* From
before the foundation of the world
He surrenders begotten Deity back to
begetting Deity in obedience. And as
the Son glorifies the Father, so also
the Father glorifies the Son.† And,
with submission, as becomes a lay-
man, I think it was truly said 'God
loveth not Himself as Himself but as

---

*George MacDonald, *Unspoken Sermons:
3rd Series,* pp. 11, 12.
†John 17:1, 4, 5.

Goodness; and if there were aught better than God, He would love that and not Himself'.* From the highest to the lowest, self exists to be abdicated and, by that abdication, becomes the more truly self, to be thereupon yet the more abdicated, and so forever. This is not a heavenly law which we can escape by remaining earthly, nor an earthly law which we can escape by being saved. What is outside the system of self-giving is not earth, nor nature, nor 'ordinary life', but simply and solely hell. Yet

---

* *Theol. Germ.,* xxxii.

even hell derives from this law such
reality as it has. That fierce imprison-
ment in the self is but the obverse
of the self-giving which is absolute
reality; the negative shape which the
outer darkness takes by surrounding
and defining the shape of the real, or
which the real imposes on the darkness by having a shape and positive
nature of its own.

The golden apple of selfhood,
thrown among the false gods, became
an apple of discord because they
scrambled for it. They did not know
the first rule of the holy game, which
is that every player must by all means

touch the ball and then immediately pass it on. To be found with it in your hands is a fault: to cling to it, death. But when it flies to and fro among the players too swift for eye to follow, and the great master Himself leads the revelry, giving Himself eternally to His creatures in the generation, and back to Himself in the sacrifice, of the Word, then indeed the eternal dance 'makes heaven drowsy with the harmony'. All pains and pleasures we have known on earth are early initiations in the movements of that dance: but the dance itself is strictly incomparable

with the sufferings of this present
time. As we draw nearer to its un-
created rhythm, pain and pleasure
sink almost out of sight. There is joy
in the dance, but it does not exist
for the sake of joy. It does not even
exist for the sake of good, or of love.
It is Love Himself, and Good Himself, and therefore happy. It does
not exist for us, but we for it. The
size and emptiness of the universe
which frightened us at the outset of
this book, should awe us still, for
though they may be no more than a
subjective by-product of our three-
dimensional imagining, yet they

symbolise great truth. As our Earth is
to all the stars, so doubtless are we
men and our concerns to all creation;
as all the stars are to space itself, so are
all creatures, all thrones and powers
and mightiest of the created gods, to
the abyss of the self-existing Being,
who is to us Father and Redeemer
and indwelling Comforter, but of
whom no man nor angel can say nor
conceive what He is in and for Himself, or what is the work that he
'maketh from the beginning to the
end'. For they are all derived and un-
substantial things. Their vision fails

them and they cover their eyes from
the intolerable light of utter actuality,
which was and is and shall be, which
never could have been otherwise,
which has no opposite.

3

THE WEIGHT

OF GLORY

I F YOU ASKED twenty good men today what they thought the highest of the virtues, nineteen of them would reply, Unselfishness. But if you had asked almost any of the great Christians of old, he would have replied, Love. You see what has happened? A negative term has been substituted for a positive, and this is of more than philological importance. The negative idea of Unselfishness carries with it the suggestion not primarily of securing

45

good things for others, but of going without them ourselves, as if our abstinence and not their happiness was the important point. I do not think this is the Christian virtue of Love. The New Testament has lots to say about self-denial, but not about self-denial as an end in itself. We are told to deny ourselves and to take up our crosses in order that we may follow Christ; and nearly every description of what we shall ultimately find if we do so contains an appeal to desire. If there lurks in most modern minds the notion that to desire our own good

and earnestly to hope for the enjoyment of it is a bad thing, I submit
that this notion has crept in from
Kant and the Stoics and is no part of
the Christian faith. Indeed, if we
consider the unblushing promises of
reward and the staggering nature of
the rewards promised in the Gospels,
it would seem that Our Lord finds
our desires not too strong, but too
weak. We are half-hearted creatures,
fooling about with drink and sex and
ambition when infinite joy is offered
us, like an ignorant child who wants
to go on making mud pies in a slum

because he cannot imagine what is meant by the offer of a holiday at the sea. We are far too easily pleased.

We must not be troubled by unbelievers when they say that this promise of reward makes the Christian life a mercenary affair. There are different kinds of rewards. There is the reward which has no natural connection with the things you do to earn it and is quite foreign to the desires that ought to accompany those things. Money is not the natural reward of love; that is why we call a man mercenary if he marries a woman for the sake of her money. But marriage is

the proper reward for a real lover, and
he is not mercenary for desiring it. A
general who fights well in order to
get a peerage is mercenary; a general
who fights for victory is not, victory
being the proper reward of battle as
marriage is the proper reward of love.
The proper rewards are not simply
tacked on to the activity for which
they are given, but are the activity
itself in consummation. There is also
a third case, which is more complicated. An enjoyment of Greek poetry
is certainly a proper, and not a mercenary, reward for learning Greek;
but only those who have reached the

stage of enjoying Greek poetry can tell from their own experience that this is so. The schoolboy beginning Greek grammar cannot look forward to his adult enjoyment of Sophocles as a lover looks forward to marriage or a general to victory. He has to begin by working for marks, or to escape punishment, or to please his parents, or, at best, in the hope of a future good which he cannot at present imagine or desire. His position, therefore, bears a certain resemblance to that of the mercenary; the reward he is going to get will, in actual fact, be a natural or proper reward, but he

will not know that till he has got it.
Of course, he gets it gradually; enjoyment creeps in upon the mere
drudgery, and nobody could point
to a day or an hour when the one
ceased and the other began. But it is
just insofar as he approaches the reward that he becomes able to desire
it for its own sake; indeed, the power
of so desiring it is itself a preliminary
reward.

The Christian, in relation to
heaven, is in much the same position
as this schoolboy. Those who have attained everlasting life in the vision of
God doubtless know very well that it

is no mere bribe, but the very consummation of their earthly disciple-
ship; but we who have not yet
attained it cannot know this in the
same way, and cannot even begin to
know it at all except by continuing to
obey and finding the first reward of
our obedience in our increasing
power to desire the ultimate reward.
Just in proportion as the desire
grows, our fear lest it should be a
mercenary desire will die away and
finally be recognised as an absurdity.
But probably this will not, for most
of us, happen in a day; poetry replaces grammar, gospel replaces law,

longing transforms obedience, as gradually as the tide lifts a grounded ship.

But there is one other important similarity between the schoolboy and ourselves. If he is an imaginative boy, he will, quite probably, be revelling in the English poets and romancers suitable to his age some time before he begins to suspect that Greek grammar is going to lead him to more and more enjoyments of this same sort. He may even be neglecting his Greek to read Shelley and Swinburne in secret. In other words, the desire which Greek is really going to gratify

already exists in him and is attached
to objects which seem to him quite
unconnected with Xenophon and
the verbs in [Greek]. Now, if we are
made for heaven, the desire for our
proper place will be already in us, but
not yet attached to the true object,
and will even appear as the rival of
that object. And this, I think, is just
what we find. No doubt there is one
point in which my analogy of the
schoolboy breaks down. The English
poetry which he reads when he
ought to be doing Greek exercises
may be just as good as the Greek
poetry to which the exercises are

leading him, so that in fixing on
Milton instead of journeying on to
Aeschylus his desire is not embracing
a false object. But our case is very different. If a transtemporal, transfinite
good is our real destiny, then any
other good on which our desire fixes
must be in some degree fallacious,
must bear at best only a symbolical
relation to what will truly satisfy.

In speaking of this desire for our
own far-off country, which we find
in ourselves even now, I feel a certain
shyness. I am almost committing an
indecency. I am trying to rip open
the inconsolable secret in each one of

you—the secret which hurts so much that you take your revenge on it by calling it names like Nostalgia and Romanticism and Adolescence; the secret also which pierces with such sweetness that when, in very intimate conversation, the mention of it becomes imminent, we grow awkward and affect to laugh at ourselves; the secret we cannot hide and cannot tell, though we desire to do both. We cannot tell it because it is a desire for something that has never actually appeared in our experience. We cannot hide it because our experience is constantly suggesting it, and we betray ourselves like lovers at the mention of a name. Our commonest expedient is to call it beauty and behave as if that had settled the matter. Wordsworth's expedient was to identify it with certain moments in his own past. But all this is a cheat. If Wordsworth had gone back to those moments in the past, he would not have found the thing itself, but only the reminder of it; what he remembered would turn out to be itself a remembering. The books or the music in which we thought the beauty was located will betray us if we trust to them; it was not *in* them,

it only came *through* them, and what
came through them was longing.
These things—the beauty, the mem-
ory of our own past—are good im-
ages of what we really desire; but if
they are mistaken for the thing itself,
they turn into dumb idols, breaking
the hearts of their worshippers. For
they are not the thing itself; they are
only the scent of a flower we have
not found, the echo of a tune we
have not heard, news from a country
we have never yet visited. Do you
think I am trying to weave a spell?
Perhaps I am; but remember your
fairy tales. Spells are used for breaking

enchantments as well as for inducing
them. And you and I have need of
the strongest spell that can be found
to wake us from the evil enchantment
of worldliness which has been laid
upon us for nearly a hundred years.
Almost our whole education has
been directed to silencing this shy,
persistent, inner voice; almost all our
modern philosophies have been de-
vised to convince us that the good of
man is to be found on this earth. And
yet it is a remarkable thing that such
philosophies of Progress or Creative
Evolution themselves bear reluctant
witness to the truth that our real goal

is elsewhere. When they want to convince you that earth is your home, notice how they set about it. They begin by trying to persuade you that earth can be made into heaven, thus giving a sop to your sense of exile in earth as it is. Next, they tell you that this fortunate event is still a good way off in the future, thus giving a sop to your knowledge that the fatherland is not here and now. Finally, lest your longing for the transtemporal should awake and spoil the whole affair, they use any rhetoric that comes to hand to keep out of your mind the recollection

that even if all the happiness they
promised could come to man on
earth, yet still each generation would
lose it by death, including the last
generation of all, and the whole story
would be nothing, not even a story,
for ever and ever. Hence all the non-
sense that Mr. Shaw puts into the
final speech of Lilith, and Bergson's
remark that the *élan vital* is capable
of surmounting all obstacles, perhaps
even death—as if we could believe
that any social or biological develop-
ment on this planet will delay the
senility of the sun or reverse the
second law of thermodynamics.

Do what they will, then, we remain conscious of a desire which
no natural happiness will satisfy. But
is there any reason to suppose that
reality offers any satisfaction to it?
"Nor does the being hungry prove
that we have bread." But I think it
may be urged that this misses the
point. A man's physical hunger does
not prove that man will get any
bread; he may die of starvation on a
raft in the Atlantic. But surely a man's
hunger does prove that he comes of a
race which repairs its body by eating
and inhabits a world where eatable
substances exist. In the same way,

though I do not believe (I wish I did) that my desire for Paradise proves that I shall enjoy it, I think it a pretty good indication that such a thing exists and that some men will. A man may love a woman and not win her; but it would be very odd if the phenomenon called "falling in love" occurred in a sexless world.

Here, then, is the desire, still wandering and uncertain of its object and still largely unable to see that object in the direction where it really lies. Our sacred books give us some account of the object. It is, of course, a symbolical account. Heaven is, by

definition, outside our experience,
but all intelligible descriptions must
be of things within our experience.
The scriptural picture of heaven is
therefore just as symbolical as the picture which our desire, unaided, in-
vents for itself; heaven is not really
full of jewellery any more than it is
really the beauty of Nature, or a fine
piece of music. The difference is that
the scriptural imagery has authority.
It comes to us from writers who were
closer to God than we, and it has
stood the test of Christian experience
down the centuries. The natural appeal of this authoritative imagery is

to me, at first, very small. At first sight it chills, rather than awakes, my desire. And that is just what I ought to expect. If Christianity could tell me no more of the far-off land than my own temperament led me to surmise already, then Christianity would be no higher than myself. If it has more to give me, I expect it to be less immediately attractive than "my own stuff." Sophocles at first seems dull and cold to the boy who has only reached Shelley. If our religion is something objective, then we must never avert our eyes from those elements in it which seem puzzling or repellent; for it will be precisely the puzzling or the repellent which conceals what we do not yet know and need to know.

The promises of Scripture may very roughly be reduced to five heads. It is promised (1) that we shall be with Christ; (2) that we shall be like Him; (3) with an enormous wealth of imagery, that we shall have "glory"; (4) that we shall, in some sense, be fed or feasted or entertained; and (5) that we shall have some sort of official position in the universe—ruling cities, judging angels, being pillars of God's temple. The first question I ask about these promises is "Why any one of them except the first?" Can anything be added to the conception of being with Christ? For it must be true, as an old writer says, that he who has God and everything else has no more than he who has God only. I think the answer turns again on the nature of symbols. For though it may escape our notice at first glance, yet it is true that any conception of being with Christ which most of us can now form will be not very much less symbolical than the other promises; for it will smuggle in ideas of proximity in space and loving

conversation as we now understand
conversation, and it will probably
concentrate on the humanity of
Christ to the exclusion of His deity.
And, in fact, we find that those
Christians who attend solely to this
first promise always do fill it up with
very earthly imagery indeed—in fact,
with hymeneal or erotic imagery. I
am not for a moment condemning
such imagery. I heartily wish I could
enter into it more deeply than I do,
and pray that I yet shall. But my point
is that this also is only a symbol, like
the reality in some respects, but unlike it in others, and therefore needs

correction from the different symbols
in the other promises. The variation
of the promises does not mean that
anything other than God will be our
ultimate bliss; but because God is
more than a Person, and lest we
should imagine the joy of His presence too exclusively in terms of our
present poor experience of personal
love, with all its narrowness and strain
and monotony, a dozen changing im-
ages, correcting and relieving each
other, are supplied.

I turn next to the idea of glory.
There is no getting away from the fact
that this idea is very prominent in the

New Testament and in early Christian writings. Salvation is constantly associated with palms, crowns, white robes, thrones, and splendour like the sun and stars. All this makes no immediate appeal to me at all, and in that respect I fancy I am a typical modern. Glory suggests two ideas to me, of which one seems wicked and the other ridiculous. Either glory means to me fame, or it means luminosity. As for the first, since to be famous means to be better known than other people, the desire for fame appears to me as a competitive passion and therefore of hell rather than heaven. As for the second, who wishes to become a kind of living electric light bulb?

When I began to look into this matter I was shocked to find such different Christians as Milton, Johnson, and Thomas Aquinas taking heavenly glory quite frankly in the sense of fame or good report. But not fame conferred by our fellow creatures— fame with God, approval or (I might say) "appreciation" by God. And then, when I had thought it over, I saw that this view was scriptural; nothing can eliminate from the parable the divine *accolade,* "Well done, thou good and

faithful servant." With that, a good
deal of what I had been thinking all
my life fell down like a house of
cards. I suddenly remembered that no
one can enter heaven except as a
child; and nothing is so obvious in a
child—not in a conceited child, but
in a good child—as its great and
undisguised pleasure in being praised.
Not only in a child, either, but even
in a dog or a horse. Apparently
what I had mistaken for humility
had, all these years, prevented me
from understanding what is in fact
the humblest, the most childlike, the
most creaturely of pleasures—nay,

the specific pleasure of the inferior:
the pleasure of a beast before men, a
child before its father, a pupil before
his teacher, a creature before its
Creator. I am not forgetting how
horribly this most innocent desire is
parodied in our human ambitions,
or how very quickly, in my own experience, the lawful pleasure of praise
from those whom it was my duty to
please turns into the deadly poison
of self-admiration. But I thought I
could detect a moment—a very, very
short moment—before this happened, during which the satisfaction
of having pleased those whom I

rightly loved and rightly feared was pure. And that is enough to raise our thoughts to what may happen when the redeemed soul, beyond all hope and nearly beyond belief, learns at last that she has pleased Him whom she was created to please. There will be no room for vanity then. She will be free from the miserable illusion that it is her doing. With no taint of what we should now call self-approval she will most innocently rejoice in the thing that God has made her to be, and the moment which heals her old inferiority complex forever will also drown her pride deeper than

Prospero's book. Perfect humility dispenses with modesty. If God is satisfied with the work, the work may be satisfied with itself; "it is not for her to bandy compliments with her Sovereign." I can imagine someone saying that he dislikes my idea of heaven as a place where we are patted on the back. But proud misunderstanding is behind that dislike. In the end that Face which is the delight or the terror of the universe must be turned upon each of us either with one expression or with the other, either conferring glory inexpressible or inflicting shame that can never be cured or disguised. I read in a periodical the other day that the fundamental thing is how we think of God. By God Himself, it is not! How God thinks of us is not only more important, but infinitely more important. Indeed, how we think of Him is of no importance except insofar as it is related to how He thinks of us. It is written that we shall "stand before" Him, shall appear, shall be inspected. The promise of glory is the promise, almost incredible and only possible by the work of Christ, that some of us, that any of us who really chooses, shall actually survive that examina-

tion, shall find approval, shall please
God. To please God . . . to be a real
ingredient in the divine happiness . . .
to be loved by God, not merely
pitied, but delighted in as an artist de-
lights in his work or a father in a
son—it seems impossible, a weight or
burden of glory which our thoughts
can hardly sustain. But so it is.

And now notice what is happen-
ing. If I had rejected the authoritative
and scriptural image of glory and
stuck obstinately to the vague desire
which was, at the outset, my only
pointer to heaven, I could have seen
no connection at all between that

desire and the Christian promise. But now, having followed up what seemed puzzling and repellent in the sacred books, I find, to my great surprise, looking back, that the connection is perfectly clear. Glory, as Christianity teaches me to hope for it, turns out to satisfy my original desire and indeed to reveal an element in that desire which I had not noticed. By ceasing for a moment to consider my own wants I have begun to learn better what I really wanted. When I attempted, a few minutes ago, to describe our spiritual longings, I was omitting one of their most

curious characteristics. We usually
notice it just as the moment of vision
dies away, as the music ends, or as the
landscape loses the celestial light.
What we feel then has been well
described by Keats as "the journey
homeward to habitual self." You
know what I mean. For a few minutes we have had the illusion of be-
longing to that world. Now we wake
to find that it is no such thing. We
have been mere spectators. Beauty
has smiled, but not to welcome us;
her face was turned in our direction,
but not to see us. We have not been
accepted, welcomed, or taken into

the dance. We may go when we
please, we may stay if we can: "Nobody marks us." A scientist may reply
that since most of the things we call
beautiful are inanimate, it is not very
surprising that they take no notice of
us. That, of course, is true. It is not
the physical objects that I am speaking of, but that indescribable something of which they become for a
moment the messengers. And part of
the bitterness which mixes with the
sweetness of that message is due to
the fact that it so seldom seems to be
a message intended for us, but rather
something we have overheard. By

bitterness I mean pain, not resent-
ment. We should hardly dare to ask
that any notice be taken of ourselves.
But we pine. The sense that in this
universe we are treated as strangers,
the longing to be acknowledged, to
meet with some response, to bridge
some chasm that yawns between us
and reality, is part of our inconsolable
secret. And surely, from this point
of view, the promise of glory, in the
sense described, becomes highly rele-
vant to our deep desire. For glory
means good report with God, accept-
ance by God, response, acknowledgement, and welcome into the heart of

things. The door on which we have been knocking all our lives will open at last.

Perhaps it seems rather crude to describe glory as the fact of being "noticed" by God. But this is almost the language of the New Testament. St. Paul promises to those who love God not, as we should expect, that they will know Him, but that they will be known by Him (1 Cor. 8:3). It is a strange promise. Does not God know all things at all times? But it is dreadfully re-echoed in another passage of the New Testament. There we are warned that it may happen to

anyone of us to appear at last before
the face of God and hear only the
appalling words, "I never knew you.
Depart from Me." In some sense, as
dark to the intellect as it is unen-
durable to the feelings, we can be
both banished from the presence of
Him who is present everywhere and
erased from the knowledge of Him
who knows all. We can be left utterly
and absolutely *outside*—repelled,
exiled, estranged, finally and un-
speakably ignored. On the other
hand, we can be called in, welcomed,
received, acknowledged. We walk
every day on the razor edge between

these two incredible possibilities. Apparently, then, our lifelong nostalgia, our longing to be reunited with something in the universe from which we now feel cut off, to be on the inside of some door which we have always seen from the outside, is no mere neurotic fancy, but the truest index of our real situation. And to be at last summoned inside would be both glory and honour beyond all our merits and also the healing of that old ache.

And this brings me to the other sense of glory—glory as brightness, splendour, luminosity. We are to

shine as the sun, we are to be given
the Morning Star. I think I begin to
see what it means. In one way, of
course, God has given us the Morning Star already: you can go and
enjoy the gift on many fine mornings
if you get up early enough. What
more, you may ask, do we want? Ah,
but we want so much more—something the books on aesthetics take
little notice of. But the poets and the
mythologies know all about it. We
do not want merely to *see* beauty,
though, God knows, even that is
bounty enough. We want something
else which can hardly be put into

words—to be united with the beauty we see, to pass into it, to receive it into ourselves, to bathe in it, to become part of it. That is why we have peopled air and earth and water with gods and goddesses and nymphs and elves—that, though we cannot, yet these projections can enjoy in themselves that beauty, grace, and power of which Nature is the image. That is why the poets tell us such lovely falsehoods. They talk as if the west wind could really sweep into a human soul; but it can't. They tell us that "beauty born of murmuring sound" will pass into a human face;

but it won't. Or not yet. For if we
take the imagery of Scripture seriously, if we believe that God will one
day *give* us the Morning Star and
cause us to *put on* the splendour of
the sun, then we may surmise that
both the ancient myths and the modern poetry, so false as history, may be
very near the truth as prophecy. At
present we are on the outside of the
world, the wrong side of the door.
We discern the freshness and purity
of morning, but they do not make us
fresh and pure. We cannot mingle
with the splendours we see. But all
the leaves of the New Testament are

rustling with the rumour that it will not always be so. Some day, God willing, we shall get *in*. When human souls have become as perfect in voluntary obedience as the inanimate creation is in its lifeless obedience, then they will put on its glory, or rather that greater glory of which Nature is only the first sketch. For you must not think that I am putting forward any heathen fancy of being absorbed into Nature. Nature is mortal; we shall outlive her. When all the suns and nebulae have passed away, each one of you will still be alive. Nature is only the image, the symbol; but it is the symbol Scripture invites me to use. We are summoned to pass in through Nature, beyond her, into that splendour which she fitfully reflects.

And in there, in beyond Nature, we shall eat of the tree of life. At present, if we are reborn in Christ, the spirit in us lives directly on God; but the mind and, still more, the body receives life from Him at a thousand removes—through our ancestors, through our food, through the elements. The faint, far-off results of those energies which God's creative rapture implanted in matter when He made the worlds are what we now call physical pleasures; and even thus filtered, they are too much for our present management. What would it be to taste at the fountain-head that stream of which even these lower reaches prove so intoxicating? Yet that, I believe, is what lies before us. The whole man is to drink joy from the fountain of joy. As St. Augustine said, the rapture of the saved soul will "flow over" into the glorified body. In the light of our present specialised and depraved appetites, we cannot imagine this *torrens voluptatis,* and I warn everyone most seriously not to try. But it must be

mentioned, to drive out thoughts
even more misleading—thoughts that
what is saved is a mere ghost, or that
the risen body lives in numb insensi-
bility. The body was made for the
Lord, and these dismal fancies are
wide of the mark.

Meanwhile the cross comes before
the crown and tomorrow is a Mon-
day morning. A cleft has opened in
the pitiless walls of the world, and we
are invited to follow our great Cap-
tain inside. The following Him is,
of course, the essential point. That
being so, it may be asked what practi-
cal use there is in the speculations

which I have been indulging. I can think of at least one such use. It may be possible for each to think too much of his own potential glory hereafter; it is hardly possible for him to think too often or too deeply about that of his neighbour. The load, or weight, or burden of my neighbour's glory should be laid on my back, a load so heavy that only humility can carry it, and the backs of the proud will be broken. It is a serious thing to live in a society of possible gods and goddesses, to remember that the dullest and most uninteresting person you can talk to may one day be a creature

which, if you say it now, you would
be strongly tempted to worship, or
else a horror and a corruption such as
you now meet, if at all, only in a
nightmare. All day long we are, in
some degree, helping each other to
one or other of these destinations. It
is in the light of these overwhelming
possibilities, it is with the awe and the
circumspection proper to them, that
we should conduct all our dealings
with one another, all friendships, all
loves, all play, all politics. There are
no *ordinary* people. You have never
talked to a mere mortal. Nations, cul-
tures, arts, civilisations—these are

mortal, and their life is to ours as the life of a gnat. But it is immortals whom we joke with, work with, marry, snub, and exploit—immortal horrors or everlasting splendours. This does not mean that we are to be perpetually solemn. We must play. But our merriment must be of that kind (and it is, in fact, the merriest kind) which exists between people who have, from the outset, taken each other seriously—no flippancy, no superiority, no presumption. And our charity must be a real and costly love, with deep feeling for the sins in spite of which we love the sinner—

no mere tolerance, or indulgence
which parodies love as flippancy
parodies merriment. Next to the
Blessed Sacrament itself, your neighbour is the holiest object presented to
your senses. If he is your Christian
neighbour, he is holy in almost the
same way, for in him also Christ *vere
latitat*—the glorifier and the glorified,
Glory Himself, is truly hidden.

MADE

FOR

HEAVEN